MEDICAL MEDIUM

THYROID HEALING

Diet

Smoothie

Over 60 Healthy and Delicious Recipes to Help Combat Hashimoto's Thyroiditis and Other Thyroid Issue

By
Lizzy Brown

.... MEDICAL MEDIUM ....

Copyright © 2019, By Lizzy Brown
ISBN-13: 978-1-950772-47-6
ISBN-10: 1-950772-47-0

All Rights Reserved. No part of this publication may be reproduced in any form or by any means, including scanning, photocopying, or otherwise without prior written permission of the copyright holder.

Disclaimer:

The information provided in this book is designed to provide helpful information on the subjects discussed. The publisher and author are not responsible for any specific health or allergy needs that may require medical supervision and are not liable for any damages or negative consequences from any treatment, action, application or preparation, to any person reading or following the information in this book.

Table of Contents

INTRODUCTION: 6
    An Overview on Hashimoto's thyroiditis? 6
    The Root Causes of Hashimoto's Thyroiditis? 7
        What are the risk factors for Hashimoto's thyroiditis? 7
        Signs and Symptoms of Hashimoto's thyroiditis 8
        What are the complications of Hashimoto's thyroiditis? 9
RECIPES TO HELP COMBAT HASHIMOTO'S THYROIDITIS 11
    Strawberry Vanilla Coconut Smoothie 11
    Tropical Cocktail 12
    CILANTRO WITH SPINACH SMOOTHIE 13
    KIWI AND APPLE GREEN SMOOTHIE 14
    COCONUT, APPLE AND YOGURT GREEN SMOOTHIE 15
    CHOCOLATE COVERED CHERRY GREEN SMOOTHIES 16
    RAW CHOCOLATE ALMOND GREEN SMOOTHIE 17
    AVOCADO GREEN SMOOTHIE 18
    DATES AND CASHEWS GREEN SMOOTHIE 19
    Energy Berry Smoothie 20
    Fresh Fruity Smoothie with Coconut Oil 21
    Fruit-Coconut Smoothie 22
    Fruity Tropical Smoothie 23
    Get Your Greens Smoothie 24
    Hot Cocoa 25
    Iced Coconut Mocha Cappuccino 26
    Hot Fudge Sauce 27
    Non-Dairy Coconut-Mocha Coffee Creamer 28
    Pecan Coconut Chocolate Milk 29
    Carrot Coconut Candy 29
    Ingredients: 29

- 2 cups of whole organic cane sugar 29
- Post-Holiday Power Smoothie 31
- Quick Tropical Coconut Smoothie 32
- Raspberries & Cream Breakfast Smoothie... 33
- Raspberry Coconut Smoothie.. 34
- Raspberry Peach Melba Smoothie 36
- Rise & Shine Breakfast Smoothie... 37
- Sensational Banana Strawberry Smoothie 37
- Strawberries & Coconut Cream Protein Shake 38
- Strawberry Coconut Bliss Smoothie 39
- Strawberry Lemon Coconut Smoothie 40
- Avocado Shake Recipe:.. 41
- Avocado-Banana Smoothie.. 42
- Avocado Milkshake 43
- Avocado Shake or Smoothie 44
- Chocolate!! Avocado Paleo Smoothie Recipe 45
- Avocado Chocolate Peanut Butter Smoothie... 46
- Chocolate Avocado Strawberry Smoothie Recipe.. 48
- Avocado Berry Banana Breakfast Smoothie 48
- Avocado Mango Smoothie 49
- Avocado, Mango, and Pineapple Smoothie 50
- Avocado Mango Lime Smoothie Recipe.. 51
- Mango Banana Avocado Smoothie with Chia Seeds 53
- Banana Orange Smoothie 53
- Nourishing Pumpkin Smoothie... 54
- Matcha Latte 55
- Ginger and Mint Strawberry Cobbler 56
- Spinach Peach Smoothie 57
- Silky Choco-Hazelnut Smoothie 58
- super green Basil Smoothie 59

- Balancing Pumpkin Smoothie 60
- Turmeric Chai Latte (dairy free) 61
- Better Than Coffee (Chicory Latte) 63
- Goji Grapefruit Parsley Smoothie 64
- Blackberry Power Smoothie 65
- Chocolate Addiction Smoothie with Avocado and Cacao Powder 67
- Strawberry Lemon Coconut Smoothie 68
- Strawberry Mango Coconut Delight 69
- Breakfast in a Cup 70
- Caramelized Tropical Peach Smoothie 70
- Cashew Coconut Creamer (Dairy free) 71
- Chocolate Coconut Banana Protein Shake 72
- Chocolate Coconut Smoothie 73
- Coconut Blueberry Smoothie 75
- Coconut Cream Mocha 75
- Coconut Date Shake 76
- Coconut Eggnog Smoothie 78
- Coconut Fruit Smoothie 79
- Coconut Latté 80
- Coconut Peanut Butter Banana Protein Shake 81
- Coconut Pumpkin Pie Smoothie 81
- Coconut Smoothie 82
- Coconut Tropical Bliss Smoothie 83
- Coco nutty Green Smoothie 84
- Creamy Coconut Cinnamon Smoothie 85
- Dark Chocolate Raspberry Custard Smoothie 86

CONCLUSION 87

INTRODUCTION:

An Overview on Hashimoto's thyroiditis?

Hashimoto's thyroiditis or Hashimoto's disease is a disease affecting the thyroid gland. This is the most common cause of hypothyroidism in the United States. in persons older than 6 years. Often in women than in men. The maximum age for women to leave is between 30 and 50; Majority of men who are affected usually develop the condition 10-15 years later.

The name comes from a medical researcher who first described the microscopic characteristics of the disease in 1912. Hashimoto's thyroiditis is an autoimmune disease in which the immune system attacks the thyroid gland. Thyroid hormone levels are usually checked every 6 to 12 weeks when the drug is actively adjusted and stabilized 6-12 months later. If side effects occur, I suggest you should follow with your doctor.

Prospects for those with Hashimoto's thyroiditis are good. Although long-term substitution of thyroid hormone therapy is probably needed, along with regular blood tests and monitoring of symptoms, the side effects are minimal, and the long-term prognosis is good.

The Root Causes of Hashimoto's Thyroiditis?

Hashimoto's cause is considered a combination of genetic predisposition to the process triggers an environment that begins with autoimmune destruction. What really boosts the immune response to the thyroid gland remains unknown. Other factors, including heredity, gender, and age, also play a role in the development of this disorder.

Normally, the immune system functions to protect against viruses, bacteria, and foreign substances (antigens) that attack the body. In the case of an autoimmune disease, the immune system mistakenly attacks body parts. In the case of Hashimoto's thyroiditis, the immune system attacks the thyroid gland.

The autoimmune process causes thyroiditis, which causes a change in the ability of the thyroid to create hormones, leading to hypothyroidism. The pituitary gland reacts with increasing TSH and is trying to boost the thyroid gland to produce more thyroid hormones. This can cause the growth of the gland.

What are the risk factors for Hashimoto's thyroiditis?

Radiation exposure has been shown to increase the likelihood of developing autoantibodies in the thyroid gland.

People who develop this disease often have a family history of Hashimoto's thyroiditis or other autoimmune disorders.

Women are 10 to 15 times more likely than men to develop Hashimoto's thyroiditis.

Excess intake of iodine is associated with higher prevalence of Hashimoto thyroiditis than in people with mild lack of iodine.

Signs and Symptoms of Hashimoto's thyroiditis

Signs and symptoms of Hashimoto's thyroiditis are the same as for hypothyroidism. The disease is a slow progression and the onset of the symptoms is gradual. It could take years for true hypothyroidism to continue to develop.

The signs and symptoms of hypothyroidism vary considerably, depending on the strength of the lack of hormones. Some of the complaints experienced by those suffering from hypothyroidism include:

These signs and symptoms may increase in weight as the disease worsens.

1. Mist fog and forget
2. Tiredness
3. Feeling of excessive cold
4. Dry skin
5. Fluid retention
6. Non-specific pain and stiffness of the muscles and joints
7. Excessive or prolonged menstrual bleeding (menorrhagia)
8. Depression
9. Yarn weight
10. Pockets on the face
11. Infertility (difficulty gaining pregnancy)
12. Dilution, breakage hair

13. Hair loss
14. Slow heart
15. Irregular menstrual periods
16. Reduction of sweating (sweating)
17. thick or fragile nails
18. Reduced reflex
19. Swelling of hands and feet
20. Cold skin
21. hangover

What are the complications of Hashimoto's thyroiditis?

Hashimoto's thyroiditis complications are similar to those in the inactive thyroid gland.

Cardiac complications: Long-term hypothyroidism that may arise from untreated thyroiditis may also be associated with an increased risk of heart disease. Heart disease may be directly associated with hypothyroid effects in the heart, resulting in changes in the contraction and rhythm that can lead to subsequent heart failure. There are also indirect effects, such as hypercholesterolemia (increasing "bad" cholesterol is often seen with hypothyroidism).

Psychiatric complications: Depression can occur early in Hashimoto's thyroid disease and if there is a fundamental depression, adding Hashimoto can aggravate the condition. Patients may complain of mental fog or slow reaction time, and sexual desire is often observed.

Myxedema coma: In its most difficult form, untreated hypothyroidism can result in a rare life-threatening disease called myxedema or myxedema. There is mental retardation, deep lethargy, and finally come. It's a potentially fatal emergency.

Goiter: the pituitary gland will try to stimulate the production of thyroid hormone in the subtype thyroid gland affected by Hashimoto's thyroiditis. This can cause enlargement of the gland. Unlike the thyroid nodule, which grows only part of the gland, in this case, the whole gland is growing, a disease is known as goiter. Goiters glands are usually nothing more than aesthetic discomfort. However, in extreme cases, the growth of the gland can cause shock in the esophagus or vagina, which makes it difficult by swallowing and breathing.

RECIPES TO HELP COMBAT HASHIMOTO'S THYROIDITIS

Strawberry Vanilla Coconut Smoothie

Ingredients:

1 ¼ cups of coconut or organic whole raw milk

2-4 tablespoons of coconut oil, melted

1 cup of plain organic yogurt (preferably Greek or goat's milk is best!)

3 teaspoons of vanilla extract

16 large strawberries, fresh or frozen (if you using fresh add ice cubes to taste)

Directions:

1. First, you blend everything except coconut oil.

2. After which you slowly pour coconut oil in while blender is running.

3. At this point, you pour into a glass, garnish with some dried coconut or a fresh strawberry if you wish.

4. Enjoy!

Tropical Cocktail

Ingredients:

3 tablespoons of coconut concentrate

2 ripe bananas

2 teaspoons of lime juice

4 tablespoons of coconut oil, liquefied

300 ml water

1 cup of frozen mango

240 ml orange juice

6 tablespoons of vanilla yogurt

Ingredients:

1. First, you mix water and coconut cream concentrate together until well blended.

2. After which you put everything except oil in a blender and process until you get a smooth texture of a drink.

3. After that, you add oil and process again.

4. Feel free to add 3 drops of stevia to give a sweeter taste.

Note: this recipe is good for a hot sunny day!

CILANTRO WITH SPINACH SMOOTHIE

Ingredients:

9 ice cube

4 ½ bananas

2 ½ of fresh spinach

½-inch fresh ginger

1 ½ peeled lime

1 cup of fresh cilantro

Directions:

1. First, you pour the cilantro, spinach, and ice in the blender.

2. After which you blend on a high speed for a few seconds.

3. Then you add banana, ginger, and lime and blend until it is smooth.

KIWI AND APPLE GREEN SMOOTHIE

Ingredients:

2 chopped apples

Water

4 skinned kiwis

2 packed cups of spinach

Sprinkle with cinnamon (optional)

Directions:

1. First, you pour the entire ingredient in the blender and blend until well incorporated.

2. Make sure you serve immediately.

COCONUT, APPLE AND YOGURT GREEN SMOOTHIE

Ingredients:

2 peeled and chopped apple

4 tablespoons of shaved fresh coconut

2-cups of ice

2 chopped and frozen bananas

1-cup of plain Greek yogurt (low fat)

1 cup of coconut milk

2 cups of spinach

Directions:

1. First, you pour the entire ingredient in the blender and blend until very smooth.

2. Make sure you serve immediately.

CHOCOLATE COVERED CHERRY GREEN SMOOTHIES

Ingredients:

2 teaspoons cinnamon

Four bananas

4 cups unsweetened almond milk

4 cups fresh spinach

6-tablespoons cacao powder

4 cups cherries (pitted)

Direction:

1. First, you place the spinach and almond milk in the blender.
2. After which you blend until smooth.
3. Then you add the remaining fruits and blend them together.

RAW CHOCOLATE ALMOND GREEN SMOOTHIE

Ingredients:

2 bananas

2 tablespoons of ground flax seed

½ the water of a young coconut

1-cup raw organic almond milk

1 cup of filtered water

½ teaspoon of vanilla

2 cups of ice or to taste

4 tablespoons of raw organic cacao

2 tablespoons of raw organic almond butter

Pinch of salt

½ the meat of a young coconut

2 cups of fresh spinach

One pitted date

Directions:

1. First, you pour the entire ingredient in the blender (excluding the ice).
2. After which you blend for a few seconds.
3. Then you add the ice and blend until smooth.

AVOCADO GREEN SMOOTHIE

Ingredients:

2 apples

1 avocado

1 ½ cups of water

2 stock of celery

2 bananas

3 cups fresh baby spinach

Tip: if you want the green smoothie recipe to be sweeter, you add a natural sweetener, like agave, nectar, to taste.

Directions:

1. First, you put the entire ingredient in the blender (one at a time).

2. Then you blend until it is smooth.

DATES AND CASHEWS GREEN SMOOTHIE

Ingredients:

2-tablespoons of ground flaxseed

Six pitted dates

1-teaspoon vanilla

½ cup of roasted cashews

4 cups vanilla almond milk (unsweetened)

2 frozen bananas

6 cups baby spinach

Tip:

It is high in calories, but rich in its nutritional content.

Direction:

1. First, you pour the entire ingredient in a blender.
2. After which you blend until it is smooth.

Energy Berry Smoothie

Note:

Make sure that the berries & banana are frozen.

Ingredients:

1 banana

½ cup of orange juice

6 tablespoons of protein powder (it is optional)

6-8 ice cubes

2 cups of following berries, (or a mixture) blueberries, raspberries, strawberries or peaches

1 cup of rice, almond, coconut milk, hazelnut, or regular milk

1 cup of water

6-8 tablespoons virgin coconut oil, melted

Directions:

1. First, you place the entire ingredients into a blender except for oil and slowly pour oil in while blending.

2. After which you beat all ingredients for 2 -3 minutes, or until well mixed and blended.

Fresh Fruity Smoothie with Coconut Oil

Tips:

If you do not like the taste of an avocado, try putting one in this mixture and I assure you that you will not know it is there.

Ingredients:

4 medium apples, with skin (remove core)

2 peaches (remove pit)

8 oz. cups of plain yogurt

2 avocados (it is optional)

2 cups of red grapes

2 pears (remove core)

2 cups of strawberries (remove stems)

2 cups of raw milk

4 tablespoons of virgin coconut oil

Directions:

1. First, you place the entire ingredients in a blender and blend until smooth.

2. After that, if you find the smoothie thick, I suggest you add more milk until it reaches your preferred consistency.

3. Finally, you place leftover smoothie in the refrigerator to enjoy later.

Fruit-Coconut Smoothie

Ingredients:

1 ¼ cups of organic vanilla yogurt

½ cup of frozen blueberries

½ cup of melted coconut oil

2 ripe bananas

½ cup of shredded coconut

2 tablespoons of whey protein

Directions:

1. First, you put everything except oil in the blender and blend until combined.

2. After which you add the oil and process until well mixed.

Tips: If you want an even sweeter smoothie, I suggest you add 2 teaspoons of honey

Fruity Tropical Smoothie

Ingredients:

2 tablespoons of coconut flour

2 large organic bananas (peeled and mashed)

2 cups of fresh strawberries, sliced

20-24 ice cubes (it is optional)

6 tablespoons of virgin coconut oil (melted)

4 tablespoons of organic honey

2 cups of unsweetened pineapple chunks

4 organic kiwis (peeled and halved)

4 large organic mangoes (peeled and cubed)

Directions:

1. First, you combine virgin coconut oil, organic coconut flour, organic honey and mashed banana in a small bowl.

2. After that, you mix well, incorporating oil thoroughly.

3. After which you pour into a blender and add all other ingredients, except ice cubes.

4. At this point, you puree on high until well blended and then blend for another 1 minute.

5. If the mixture is too thick for your taste, I suggest you add some water, or add the ice and blend on high until ice crushed.

Get Your Greens Smoothie

Ingredients:

2 tablespoons of ground whole golden flax seed

2 scoops of Chocolate Goat Milk Protein

2 teaspoons of Virgin Coconut Oil, liquefied

2 large handful of whole spinach leaves

2 scoops of Mint Antioxidant Omega 3 Greens

3 - 4 cups of raw milk

2 frozen bananas (peeled and sliced into chunks)

Directions:

1. First, you combine the entire ingredients in a blender and then blend until smooth.

2. After that, you will find it thick, frothy & delicious!

Hot Cocoa

Ingredients:

2 tablespoons of Cocoa Powder

½ teaspoons of organic whole sugar (minimum)

2 tablespoons of Virgin Coconut Oil

Pinch of Himalayan salt

Directions:

1. First, you pour boiling water into a mug and let sit for about 20 seconds.

2. After which you empty the water and put one tablespoon full of the virgin coconut oil in it.

3. After that, it melts quickly as you stir in one tablespoonful of cocoa powder and a pinch of Himalayan salt.

4. At this point, you use a minimum of ½ teaspoon of whole organic sugar to cut the bitterness of the cocoa and then add stevia drops to taste. It is usually about 24 drops.

5. Then you pour boiling water in the cup, stir, and add cream or milk to taste.

6. Feel free to use other sweeteners can be used.

Iced Coconut Mocha Cappuccino

Ingredients:

1 cup of organic whole raw milk (or coconut milk)

2 tablespoons of coconut oil, melted (it is optional)

1 ¼ cups of cold, strong coffee (partly frozen if you wish)

4-8 ice cubes

4 tablespoons of fudge sauce, cold

Directions:

1. First, you place the entire ingredients except coconut oil in a blender and blend until well combined, pouring coconut oil into the cappuccino a steady stream.

2. After which you top with freshly whipped cream and enjoy!

Hot Fudge Sauce

Ingredients:

1 cup of cocoa powder

8 tablespoons of butter

3 teaspoons of vanilla extract

1 cup of sugar (plus 4 tablespoons)

1 ¼ cups of heavy cream

2-4 tablespoons of coconut oil

Directions:

1. First, you combine all ingredients except vanilla extract in a saucepan over medium heat.

2. Then when butter melts and is well mixed in, you turn heat up to high and bring fudge to a boil, whisking constantly.

3. After which you boil for 1 minute.

4. After that, you remove from heat and stir in vanilla.

5. Finally, you store in the refrigerator and do not eat it all at once.

Non-Dairy Coconut-Mocha Coffee Creamer

Ingredients:

2 cups of Coconut Cream Concentrate

4-6 tablespoons of organic cocoa powder

2 cups of Gold Label Virgin Coconut Oil

1 - 2 teaspoons of concentrated stevia powder or honey (or to taste)

Directions:

1. First, you gently soften or melt coconut oil and coconut cream until you can stir them.

2. After which you add sweetener and cocoa and mix until thoroughly combined.

3. Then you pour into small-lidded jars and refrigerate so it sets up properly without separating.

Directions to use:

1. You should mix one or more spoonsful of coffee or hot chocolate and then keeps well.

2. This recipe is great for traveling.

Pecan Coconut Chocolate Milk

Ingredients:

½ cup of pecans

6 tablespoons of virgin or expeller pressed coconut oil

2-4 tablespoons of raw honey

3 cups of organic whole milk

4 tablespoons of organic cocoa powder

Directions:

1. First, you add all ingredients except coconut oil to the blender.

2. After which you blend until smooth and with the blender still running, slowly drizzle melted/cool coconut oil into the mix.

3. Then you pour into a frosty mug or a large glass, fill with ice and serve.

4. Enjoy.

Carrot Coconut Candy

Ingredients:

2 cups of whole organic cane sugar

¼ teaspoon of salt

½ cup of coconut cream concentrates

2 pounds of grated carrots

½ cup of honey

2 cups of shredded coconut (divided use)

Juice and zest of four lemons

Directions:

1. First, you place the grated carrot, sugar, honey, and salt in a saucepan over medium-high heat.

2. After which you stir until the sugar melts.

3. At this point, you add the lemon juice and zest, reduce heat, and simmer uncovered for about 30 minutes until carrots are tender and juice is syrupy.

4. After that, you let cool and then you transfer mixture to a food processor along with 1 cup of the shredded coconut and the coconut cream concentrate.

5. This is the point when you process until thick paste forms.

6. In addition, you roll into truffle-sized balls and roll balls in the remaining shredded coconut.

7. Then you place on a lined baking sheet.

8. Finally, you let dry for a day on the baking sheet before placing in a covered container where they will keep up to 1 week.

Post-Holiday Power Smoothie

Tips:

This recipe is a yummy and nourishing powerhouse and it also perfect for breakfast or a picks me up that will have you back on track and going strong for hours.

Ingredients:

2-4 tablespoons of virgin coconut oil, melted

½ cup of organic rolled oats

2 teaspoons of vanilla

Dash salt

4 cups of frozen strawberries (or any frozen fruit of your choice)

3 cups of grass-fed milk, plain kefir (or coconut milk)

2 bananas, fresh or frozen

2 tablespoons of green food powder

2 tablespoons of raw honey

8 soy-free egg yolks (it is optional, but add lots of great nutrition and healthy fat for long-lasting energy)

Directions:

First, you blend the entire ingredient except the fruit until mixed after which you add fruit and then blend until smooth.

Enjoy.

Quick Tropical Coconut Smoothie

Ingredients:

4-6 large bananas, fresh or frozen

4 cups of coconut milk

4 tablespoons of coconut oil (or coconut cream concentrate)

½ cup of flax seeds

4-8 cups of pineapple juice (or preferably raw pineapple and increased coconut milk)

8-12 cups of frozen mango chunks

4-6 cups of unpacked fresh spinach or a pinch of spirulina (it is optional)

4 tablespoons of hemp hearts (or hemp protein powder)

Raw honey or dates to sweeten (optional, and usually not needed)

Directions:

1. First, you add the entire ingredients, except for any frozen fruit in a high-powered, high capacity blender.

2. At this point, if you are opting for spinach and/or dates, this is the time to add it! I usually start out on the lower end of the liquids and increase as required.

3. After which you start blender out at low speed and slowly increase to high, allowing all of the flax seeds (and spinach) to liquefy.

4. After that, you should have a large amount of liquid yummiest! To this, you will add your frozen mangoes, until your reach required amount and consistency.

5. I suggest you add purer pineapple juice to get the desired tropical flavor if it's lacking.

Note: this smoothie is creamy, sweet, and delicious!

Raspberries & Cream Breakfast Smoothie

Tips:

This recipe is rich, creamy, fruity and very filling.

Ingredients:

1 ¼ cups of milk

1 teaspoon of vanilla extract (or vanilla powder)

6-8 tablespoons of rolled oats

2-4 tablespoons of coconut oil, melted

½ cup of heavy cream

2 cups of frozen raspberries

Dash ground nutmeg

2 honey date (it is optional)

Directions

1. First, you combine the entire ingredients except for raspberries and coconut oil and let soak for about an hour or overnight.

2. After which you place the entire ingredients except for coconut oil into a blender and blend until smooth while pouring coconut oil into blender in a steady stream.

3. Finally, you pour into a glass and enjoy!

Raspberry Coconut Smoothie

Ingredients:

2 grated apple

4 tablespoons of virgin coconut oil

4 cups of unsweetened coconut milk

16 ice cubes

2 frozen bananas

2 cups of frozen raspberries

4 tablespoons of chia seeds

½ cups of unsweetened organic shredded coconut

Directions:

1. First, you place all ingredients (except ice) in the blender.

2. After which you blend on high for about 1-2 minutes.

3. After that, you add in ice cubes, blend on 'frozen drinks' mode or use ice crusher to blend cubes.

4. Then you blend until smooth.

Raspberry Peach Melba Smoothie

Tip:

This recipe is perfect for a nutritious breakfast on the go and keeps you growing strong until lunch.

Ingredients:

4-8 organic eggs OR 2-4 tablespoons of goat milk protein powder

6 tablespoons of melted virgin coconut oil

2 teaspoons of vanilla extract

3 cups of plain kefir (preferably homemade)

2 tablespoons of raw honey

1 ¼ cups of frozen raspberries

1 ¼ cups of frozen peaches

Directions:

1. First, you add kefir, eggs or protein powder, honey and coconut oil, blend to mix before frozen ingredients.

2. Finally, you add frozen fruit and vanilla, blend until smooth.

3. Make sure you serve immediately.

Rise & Shine Breakfast Smoothie

Ingredients:

2 whole mangos, fresh or frozen

2 or 4 frozen bananas

2 tablespoons of freshly ground flax seed (it is optional)

4 tablespoons of coconut oil, melted (more/less as needed)

Coconut flakes

3 cups of kefir, yogurt or buttermilk

4 handfuls of strawberries, fresh or frozen

2-6 tablespoons of raw honey

Raw egg yolks (it is optional)

Directions:

1. First, you pour your choice of cultured dairy into the blender.

2. After which you add in mangos, strawberries, bananas and honey (add flax seed and/or egg yolks if you wish).

3. After that, you give it a whirl until smooth and while it is blending, you add coconut oil and let it run for a minute more.

4. Finally, you pour into a tall, large glass and top with coconut flakes and extra ground flax seeds if you wish.

Sensational Banana Strawberry Smoothie

Ingredients:

2-4 medium strawberries + one additional strawberry for decoration (it is optional)

2 tablespoons of coconut oil, melted

6 small frozen bananas

2 ½ cups of milk

2 raw egg yolk

Directions:

1. First, you chop bananas and strawberries and put them in the blender.

2. After which you pour the milk, and egg yolk in.

3. At this point, right before you start blending pour in the coconut oil.

4. After that, you blend until smooth.

5. Finally, you pour into a glass and garnish with the extra strawberry if you wish.

6. Enjoy!

Strawberries & Coconut Cream Protein Shake

Ingredients:

2 cups of frozen strawberries (or to taste)

2 scoops of vanilla ice cream or coconut ice cream (it is optional)

2-4 tablespoons of coconut oil, melted

2 cups of whole raw milk (or coconut milk)

1 teaspoon of vanilla extract or powder

2-4 scoops of protein powder

Directions:

1. First, you place all ingredients except coconut oil into a blender and blend until smooth.

2. After which you pour coconut oil into blender in a steady stream while blending.

3. Finally, you pour into a tall glass.

4. Enjoy!

Strawberry Coconut Bliss Smoothie

Ingredients:

2-6 soy-free organic eggs

2-6 tablespoons of virgin coconut oil, melted

3-4 cups of organic frozen strawberries

3 cups of plain kefir (preferably homemade)

2 tablespoons of honey

¼ teaspoon of organic cinnamon

½ teaspoon of organic natural vanilla

Directions:

1. First, you add kefir, you needed a number of eggs, coconut oil, and honey to the blender and combine thoroughly.

2. Remember, that the extra eggs and coconut oil provide even long-lasting satisfaction and energy.

3. After that, you add vanilla, cinnamon, and strawberries.

4. After which you adjust amount according to the required thickness and blend on medium, then high speed until thoroughly combined, thick and creamy.

5. Then you garnish with additional strawberries and a sprinkle of cinnamon if you wished.

6. Serve immediately.

Strawberry Lemon Coconut Smoothie

Ingredients:

2-6 soy-free organic eggs

2-6 tablespoons of coconut oil (melted)

1 teaspoon of organic pure vanilla extract

Dashes of salt

3 cups of organic raw milk (plain kefir or milk of choice)

2 tablespoons of raw honey

2-4 cups of organic frozen strawberries (it all depends on your desired consistency)

½ teaspoon of organic lemon oil flavoring

Directions:

1. First, you put the organic raw milk, organic eggs, raw honey and coconut oil in a blender and blend thoroughly.

2. After which you add the remaining ingredients and blend until smooth. \

3. Serve immediately.

Avocado Shake Recipe:

Ingredients:

2 cups of ice (about 16 to 20 ice cubes)

½ to 1 cup of cold non-fat milk

1 ripe avocado (peeled and pitted)

½ cup of fat-free sweetened condensed milk

NOTE: Remember that the best avocados to use are those that gently yield to pressure and are free from dark blotches inside the fruit. In the other hand, it depends on how large the avocado is and how thick you want your shake.

Directions:

1. First, you scoop the avocado flesh into a blender.
2. After which you add the ice cubes, condensed milk, the least amount of non-fat milk; puree until completely smooth.
3. Then you taste and add additional milk if a thinner consistency is desired (NOTE: I prefer using the maximum amount of milk.)
4. Finally, you pour into two tall glasses and enjoy!

Avocado-Banana Smoothie

Ingredients

2 banana

3 cups of fresh orange juice (from 6 oranges)

5 to 6 cups ice

 2 avocado

1 cup of nonfat plain Greek yogurt

½ cup of honey

Directions

1. First, you combine avocado, banana, honey, yogurt, orange juice, and ice in a blender.
2. After which you blend until smooth.
3. Then you serve immediately.

Avocado Milkshake

Ingredients

2 (28 ounces) evaporated milk

6 cups of ice cubes

8 avocados

1 cup of sugar

2 teaspoons of lemon juice

Directions:

1. First, with a knife, halve avocados and remove pit.
2. After which you use a spoon, scoop flesh and cut into cubes.
3. After that, you combine avocados, milk, sugar, lemon juice and ice in a blender.
4. Then you process until smooth and blended.

Avocado Shake or Smoothie

Ingredients

4 cups of crushed ice

Honey, Agave or Sugar (6-8 tablespoons if using brown sugar), to taste

4 Avocados (preferably ripe)

2 cups of milk, plus more if needed (for Paleo sub with Almond or better still Coconut Milk)

Directions:

1. First, you place the crushed ice in a blender.
2. After which you top it with the avocado.
3. After that, you add the rest of the ingredients.
4. Then you process until smooth and thick to your desired consistency.
5. Feel free to add more milk if you want just an easy pour kind of shake (I prefer mine a little thick and creamy).
6. However, if you are feeling rather indulgent, I suggest you add some whipped cream and garnish it with a cherry on top!

Chocolate!! Avocado Paleo Smoothie Recipe

Ingredients

4 frozen bananas

4 cups of almond or better still coconut milk

2 avocados

1 cup of frozen raspberries (or better still fresh raspberries or other berries)

2-4 tablespoons of unsweetened cocoa powder

Directions:

NOTE: If you have unpeeled frozen bananas, then you should take the frozen bananas from the freezer and leave to thaw for 10 minutes before peeling (or better still cut the skin off with a paring knife).

First, you place all the ingredients into a blender and blend well.

Enjoy!

Avocado Chocolate Peanut Butter Smoothie

Ingredients

2 medium ripe frozen banana

6 tablespoons of creamy peanut butter

1 teaspoon of vanilla extract (optional, but recommended)

1 medium avocado

4 tablespoons of cocoa powder

3 cups of unsweetened vanilla almond milk (preferably more or less to desired consistency)

2 tablespoons of agave nectar, zero-calorie sweetener, or honey (more or less to taste)

Directions:

First, you add everything into a blender and blend on high for about 2 - 4 minutes, or until smooth and creamy.

Then you add more milk as necessary to reach your desired thickness.

Enjoy!

Chocolate Avocado Strawberry Smoothie Recipe

Ingredients

2 ripe avocado (roughly chopped)

3 cups of almond or better still coconut milk

Dark chocolate, grated (it is optional)

2 cups of frozen strawberries

2 tablespoons of cocoa powder

1 teaspoon of vanilla

2 tablespoons of raw honey (it is optional)

Directions:

1. First, you place all the ingredients in a blender, and pulse until everything is smooth.
2. After which you pour mix into 2 large glasses, and sprinkle grated dark chocolate on top.

Avocado Berry Banana Breakfast Smoothie

Ingredients

1 ripe frozen banana

1 cup of frozen berries

4 cups of spinach, romaine (or better still other dark leafy green)

1 ripe avocado

2 cups of nut milk or water

2/3 cup of oats

Optional: 1 or 2 Medjool dates, pitted

Directions:

1. First, you scoop the avocado flesh out of its skin, discarding the pit.
2. After which you place everything into a blender and blend until smooth and creamy.
3. Enjoy!

Notes: make sure you choose all organic ingredients if possible

Avocado Mango Smoothie

Ingredients:

1 pitted avocado

2 cups of almond milk (regular milk or coconut milk also works great)

2 cups of frozen mango

1 cup of Greek Yogurt

2-4 Tablespoons of honey

Optional add-in: 2-4 drops Orange essential oil

Directions:

First, you place all ingredients in a blender and blend until smooth.

Avocado, Mango, and Pineapple Smoothie

Ingredients

2 ripe medium avocadoes, pitted, peeled and diced (about 2 cups)

1 cup of diced pineapple (about 6 ounces)

2 tablespoons of agave nectar

1 cup of unsweetened coconut water

3 cups of diced mango (about 18 ounces)

10 ice cubes

Directions:

1. First, you add coconut water, avocado, mango, pineapple, ice, and agave nectar to blender.
2. After which you blend on high about 30 seconds until completely smooth.
3. Then you divide between two glasses and serve immediately.

Avocado Mango Lime Smoothie Recipe

Ingredients

½ avocado (peeled and seed removed)

2-4 ice cubes (it is optional)

A cup of filtered or better still spring water

½ cup of fresh (or better still frozen mango chunks)

Juice of ½ a lime

The Add-ons

½ teaspoon of ginger spice

1 tablespoon of coconut oil

½ fresh or better still frozen banana

Directions:

First, you place all of the ingredients into your blender and blend for 30-45 seconds or until the desired consistency is reached.

Mango Banana Avocado Smoothie with Chia Seeds

Ingredients

2 banana (frozen)

1 cup of Greek yogurt

Sweetener to taste (I prefer 2 tablespoons of honey)

2 cups of mango (from 2 small Ataulfo mango)

1 avocado

1 cup milk (preferably any kind you prefer)

2 tablespoons of chia seeds

Directions:

1. First, you blend all ingredients together in a food processor or blender until combined and smooth.
2. After which you add more milk for thinner consistency.
3. Then you serve immediately since avocado tends to turn brown after a while.

Banana Orange Smoothie

Ingredients:

1 cup of orange juice (more or less, depending on how thick or thin you want it)

2 tablespoons of Concentrate Coconut Cream

6 ice cubes

2 banana

6 tablespoons of virgin coconut oil, liquefied

6 tablespoons of organic whole milk vanilla yogurt

Directions:

1. First, you put the entire ingredient in a blender and blend until it is well incorporated.

2. If you wish, feel free to add 10 frozen strawberries.

Nourishing Pumpkin Smoothie

Serves: 1-2 servings

Ingredients

½ cup pumpkin (steamed and scooped out)

¼ teaspoon of pure vanilla extract

¼ inch ginger root (grated)

1 date (pitted)

¼ cup pecans

pinch of sea salt

1 tablespoon of tahini

A handful of dandelion

¼ teaspoon of cinnamon

1 tablespoon of coconut butter (however, my favored brand is Artisana)

1 tablespoon of flax seed seeds

¼ teaspoon of camu camu powder

Directions:
1. First, you put all the ingredients into a blender.
2. After which you top it up with room-temperature or warm water and give it a spin to a desired consistency.
3. Then you serve.

Matcha Latte

Equipment: blender
Serves: 2
Ingredients

1 cup of room temperature filtered water

2 tablespoons of coconut butter (preferably the Artisana brand)

2 teaspoons of maple syrup (or better still any sweetener of your choice)

¼ teaspoon of cinnamon powder (optional)

2 teaspoons of matcha tea (I use DoMatcha or Teavana brands)

½ cup of full fat coconut milk

1 cup of hot water

4 drops of liquid stevia (preferably Sweet Leaf)

¼ teaspoon of vanilla power

Directions:

1. First, you put all the ingredients in the blender but add the hot water as the last ingredient (matcha loses its enzymatic potency in high temperature).
2. After which you blend for 30 seconds and serve as a warm drink or over ice.
3. Finally, you sprinkle with cinnamon, if using.

Ginger and Mint Strawberry Cobbler

Serves: 4 to 6
Ingredients
Filling ingredients

2 tablespoons of lime juice and zest of one lime

1 tablespoon of ginger (grated)

Pinch of salt (NOTE: it will enhance the sweetness)

1 pound of strawberries

1 tablespoon of mint, finely chopped, from about 20 leaves

1 teaspoon of vanilla powder (or extract)

2 teaspoons of arrowroot (or better still tapioca starch)

Topping ingredients

½ cup of ghee or coconut oil (melted)

1 tablespoons of maple syrup

Pinch of salt

1 cup of finely shredded coconut flakes

¼ cup of arrowroot or tapioca starch

½ teaspoon of vanilla powder

Directions:

1. Meanwhile, you heat the oven to 350F.
2. After which you combine all the filling ingredients and toss to evenly cover the strawberries.
3. After that, you place in the cast iron skillet or baking dish.
4. Then you combine all the topping ingredients in a separate bowl and use your hands to work the ghee/coconut oil well into the paste until it turns into a crumble.
5. At this point, you spread the crumble evenly on top of the strawberries.
6. Finally, you bake for 30 to 40 minutes or until the topping is brown.

NOTE: feel free to replace strawberries with apples, pears or blueberries.

Spinach Peach Smoothie

Equipment: blender
Serves: 1
Ingredients

1 bunch of dandelion

½ teaspoon of star anise, ground

2 tablespoons of tahini paste (ground sesame seeds)

2 pinches of sea salt

1 bunch of spinach

1 ripe peach

½ teaspoon of vanilla powder or essence

2 tablespoons of flax seed (ground)

1 tablespoon of lemon juice

Directions:

First, you throw all ingredients into a blender and blend to desired consistency.

Silky Choco-Hazelnut Smoothie

Equipment: blender
Serves: 2
Ingredients

1 ½ tablespoons of raw cacao powder

1 teaspoon of maca powder

2 tablespoons of coconut butter

1 teaspoon of bee pollen (It is optional)

1 cup of hazelnuts

½ cup of hemp seeds

2 pitted dates

3 cups of water

Directions:

First, you blend all ingredients on high and for long enough to get a silky texture. (NOTE: if using bee pollen, I suggest you do not blend it but sprinkle it on top of the smoothie, otherwise it will become bitter).

super green Basil Smoothie

Equipment: Blender
Serves: 2

Ingredients

Handful of basil

Handful of sprouts

2 teaspoon of lime juice

¼ teaspoon of sea salt

2 cloves of garlic

½ cup of water

1 small zucchini

Handful of parsley

1 carrot

Zest from ½ lime

¼ cup of olive oil

½ teaspoon of ground cumin

¼ inch ginger root

Directions:

All you do is just blend it all up!

Balancing Pumpkin Smoothie

Serves: 1-2 depending on serving size

Ingredients

½ cup of pumpkin puree from BPA-free can or, steamed and scooped out fresh pumpkin

2 tablespoons of flax seed

¼ inch fresh ginger root (grated)

1 tablespoon of coconut butter

¼ teaspoon of pure vanilla extract

Pitch of sea salt

1½ cups of lukewarm water

¼ cup of pecans

Handful of dandelion leaves

1 tablespoon of tahini

1 date (pitted)

¼ teaspoon of cinnamon

¼ teaspoon of camu camu

Directions:

1. First, you put all the ingredients in the blender and puree until silky smooth.

Turmeric Chai Latte (dairy free)

Equipment: blender

Serves: 2

Ingredients

Masala chai mix

1 large Ceylon cinnamon stick (broken to pieces)

8 cardamom pods (crushed)

½ teaspoon of black pepper corns (crushed)

3 cups of water

2 teaspoons of rooibos or black tea

2-inch fresh ginger root (sliced)

5 cloves (crushed)

1 teaspoon fennel seed

Other ingredients

3 tablespoons of ghee or better still coconut butter

½ teaspoon of nutmeg powder (it is optional)

2 pitted dates

1 teaspoon of turmeric

¼ teaspoon of vanilla powder (it is optional)

Directions:

2. First, you place the water and the masala chai mix in the saucepan and bring water to a boil.

3. After which you reduce the heat and simmer for about 10-15 minutes.

4. After that, you strain and transfer to the blender.

5. Then you add dates and ghee and blend on high for 1 minute.

6. At this point, you add turmeric powder and blend again for a few seconds. Finally, you pour to serving glasses and sprinkle with vanilla powder and nutmeg

Better Than Coffee (Chicory Latte)

Equipment: blender, grater
Serves: 2

Ingredients

1 tablespoon of roasted dandelion root

2 tablespoons of ghee, coconut butter or butter (if tolerated)

Fresh nutmeg (nut or powder)

1 tablespoon of roasted chicory root

2 cups of water

2 pitted dates

Directions:

1. First, you place chicory and dandelion root in a cooking pot and cover with water.
2. After which you bring it to a boil, reduce the heat and simmer for 2 minutes.
3. After that, you turn off the heat and let it steep for 10 minutes.
4. Then you strain and transfers to a blender, then add the ghee and the dates.
5. Blend for about 1 minute.
6. Finally, you grate some fresh nutmeg and enjoy.
7. powder, if using.

Goji Grapefruit Parsley Smoothie

Serves: 1

Ingredients

½ grapefruit

Handful of hemp seeds

1 tablespoon of milk thistle

1 cup of filtered water

Handful of dry goji berries that have been soaked

Handful of fresh parsley

1 ½ tablespoons of ground flax seed (flax seed meal)

Handful of almonds (pecans or walnut)

Directions:

1. First, you soak the goji berries for or least two hours or overnight.
2. After which you combine all ingredients in a blender.
3. After that, you blend till either very smooth or somewhat smooth if you like chunks in your smoothie.
4. Touch your heart and tell it you love it.

Blackberry Power Smoothie

Serves: 1

Ingredients

Handful of hemp seeds

1 tablespoon of milk thistle

Handful of almonds (pecans or walnuts)

1 tablespoon of coconut oil or ghee

1 teaspoon of raw honey (it is optional)

Handful of organic blackberries

1 ½ tablespoons of ground flax seed (flax seed meal)

½ teaspoon of camu camu powder

1 cup of warm water

1 tablespoon of pumpkin seeds (it is optional)

Directions:

1. First, you combine all ingredients in a blender.

2. After which you blend till it's either very smooth or somewhat smooth if you like chunks in your smoothie.

3. Touch your heart and tell it you love it

Chocolate Addiction Smoothie with Avocado and Cacao Powder

Serves: 2

Ingredients

1 whole avocado

Handful of goji berries, presoaked for about 15 min in warm water. I suggest you use pre-soaked cherries if you are avoiding nightshades (goji is a nightshade)

Handful of raw pecan nuts

Pinch of Himalayan sea salt

Filtered water to top up the ingredients

1 tablespoon of ghee (melted)

¼ cup of raw cacao powder

1 large tablespoon of pumpkin seeds

Pinch of cinnamon

¼ teaspoon of pure vanilla extract

½ teaspoon of fresh lemon juice

Directions:

1. All you do is throw all ingredients into the blender and voila!

Strawberry Lemon Coconut Smoothie

Ingredients:

2-6 soy-free organic eggs

2-6 tablespoons of coconut oil (melted)

1 teaspoon of organic pure vanilla extract

Dashes of salt

3 cups of organic raw milk (plain kefir or milk of choice)

2 tablespoons of raw honey

2-4 cups of organic frozen strawberries (it all depends on your desired consistency)

½ teaspoon of organic lemon oil flavoring

Directions:

1. First, you put the organic raw milk, organic eggs, raw honey and coconut oil in a blender and blend thoroughly.

2. After which you add the remaining ingredients and blend until smooth. \

3. Serve immediately.

Strawberry Mango Coconut Delight

Ingredients:

8 pastured soy-free egg yolks

2 tablespoons of honey

2 cups of frozen mangos

Dashes of sea salt

3 cups of raw milk (kefir or coconut milk)

2-4 tablespoons of virgin coconut oil, melted

2 cups of frozen strawberries

2 teaspoons of vanilla extract

Directions:

1. First, you put the raw milk, egg yolks, virgin coconut oil, honey in a blender and blend until smooth.

2. After which you add remaining ingredients and blend until it reached your desired consistency.

3. Finally, you serve with additional fruit if you wish.

4. Enjoy!

Breakfast in a Cup

Ingredients:

1cup of rolled oat flakes

1 cup of coconut peanut butter (or peanut butter)

Dash cinnamon

2 cups of spinach (it is optional)

4 frozen bananas

2 cups of milk (feel free to use more or less to adjust to desired consistency)

2-4 tablespoons of coconut oil, melted

2 teaspoons of vanilla

Directions:

1. First, you place the entire ingredients in a good blender and blend until it is smooth and well mixed.

2. After which you pour into glasses and serve immediately.

Caramelized Tropical Peach Smoothie

Ingredients:

8 soy-free egg yolks (it is optional, but feel free to add lots of sustaining nutrition and energy)

4 tablespoons of coconut flakes

1 ¼ cups of frozen peaches

Dash salt

3 cups of coconut milk (plain kefir or grass-fed milk)

2 tablespoons of virgin coconut oil, melted

2 tablespoons of whole sugar (+/- to taste – remember that this is what gives it the delicious, caramelized flavor)

2 teaspoons of vanilla extract

1 cup of frozen pineapple

Directions:

1. First, you blend the entire ingredients thoroughly until smooth.

2. After which you stir in a small amount more whole sugar to each serving for a delicious caramel crunch, i.e. if you wish.

Cashew Coconut Creamer (Dairy free)

Ingredients:

½ cup of honey

4 tablespoons of coconut oil, melted (give or take as needed)

2 cups of cashew nuts (soaked overnight, rinsed)

1 teaspoon of vanilla extract

1 cup of coconut milk

Directions:

1. First, you place the entire ingredients in high-powered blender.

2. After which you blend until smooth and creamy, pouring melted coconut oil in to the mix in a steady drizzle.

3. Then you store in glass jar in the refrigerator for up to a week.

Chocolate Coconut Banana Protein Shake

Ingredients:

2 teaspoons of cocoa

½ teaspoon of guar gum (it is optional)

1 ¼ cups of water

2-6 tablespoons of coconut oil (melted)

2-4 heaping scoops of double bonded chocolate protein powder

½ teaspoon of xanthan gum (it is optional)

2 frozen bananas

1 cup of coconut milk (or organic raw whole milk)

10 ice cubes, it is optional (more or less as needed)

Directions:

1. First, you add the entire ingredients except coconut oil to blender and blend, pouring the coconut oil in slowly.

2. After which you continue blending until smooth.

Chocolate Coconut Smoothie

Ingredients:

4 tablespoons of organic golden flax seeds

2 teaspoons of organic cocoa powder

2 teaspoons of organic vanilla extract, (opt)

2 chopped pear

Ice cubes, as required

Approximately 1 ¼ cup of dates or raisins soaked in 2 cups of water

2 tablespoons of shredded (or flaked coconut)

2 - 4 teaspoons of coconut oil

2 teaspoons of organic whole sugar (or to taste)

2-4 frozen chopped bananas

Directions:

1. First, you soak the date/raisin, shredded or flaked coconut and organic golden flax seeds from 30 minutes to a couple of hours.

2. After which you blend slowly in a blender and then add other ingredients and then blend well.

3. Feel free to top this with raw cacao nibs or add other seeds/nuts as desired.

Coconut Blueberry Smoothie

Ingredients:

1 cup of organic blueberries

4 tablespoons of organic whole milk plain yogurt

12-16 ice cubes (depending on your preferred quantity)

12 oz. organic coconut milk

1 banana

2 tablespoons of virgin coconut oil

Directions:

1. First, you toss the entire ingredients in the blender and blend well until frothy.

2. Then you pour into a glass and serve.

Coconut Cream Mocha

Ingredients:

2/3 cup of sugar or honey

1 cup of water

3 - 4 cups of strong black coffee

Ice cream, of your choice for garnish (it is optional)

1 cup of cocoa powder

7 cups of whole milk

½ cup of coconut cream concentrates

4 teaspoons of vanilla extract

Whipped cream, for garnish (it is optional)

Directions:

1. First, you stir together cocoa and sweetener, in a large saucepan with a wire whisk.

2. After which you add 2 cup of milk, the water and coconut cream concentrate, over medium heat.

3. After that, you whisk and bring to a simmer.

4. At this point, you add coffee and the remaining milk and whisk until mocha is nice and hot.

5. Finally, you add vanilla.

6. Make sure you remove from heat and serve with a spoonful of the optional garnishes if you wish.

Coconut Date Shake

Ingredients:

4 tablespoons of Coconut Cream Concentrate (or preferable more to taste)

4 cups of ice (more or less depending on the desired thickness)

28 oz. of coconut milk

Small handful of dates (pits removed, more or less to taste)

4 teaspoons of coconut oil, melted

1 cup soaked almonds or Brazil nuts for extra protein (Soak for at least an hour and rinse off water).

Directions:

1. First, you place the entire ingredients in the blender.

2. While you are still blending, pour the coconut oil into the shake in a slowly.

3. After which you blend all really well for a great, healthy, non-dairy desert or breakfast drink.

Coconut Eggnog Smoothie

Ingredients:

10 large soy-free eggs

4 tablespoons of coconut cream concentrate (softened)

1 teaspoon of ground ginger

8-10 frozen ripe bananas

3 cups of raw milk (or coconut milk)

4 tablespoons of virgin coconut oil (melted)

1 teaspoon of nutmeg

1 teaspoon of cinnamon

½ teaspoon of sea salt

Directions:

1. First, you blend the entire ingredient except the bananas until thoroughly mixed.

2. After which you add the frozen bananas and blend until smooth.

3. Make sure you serve immediately with an extra sprinkle of nutmeg on top.

Coconut Fruit Smoothie

Ingredients:

1-2 whole bananas

4 tablespoons of fresh ground flax seeds

2 tablespoons of coconut oil (melted)

2 cups of coconut milk (or regular whole milk)

4 tablespoons of fresh groundnuts (such as almonds, pecans, etc.)

½ cup of frozen fruit (such as berries, peaches, etc.)

2 tablespoons of dry coconut (such as flakes, etc.)

Directions:

1. First, you place the entire ingredients except coconut oil in blender and blend.

2. After which you slowly pour coconut oil into blender while blending.

3. Then you blend until smooth and then serve.

Coconut Latté

Ingredients:

2-6 tablespoons of coconut oil

4 tablespoons of coconut flavored syrup (or preferred flavor and amount)

2-4 tablespoons of coconut cream concentrate (it is optional)

1 ¼ cups of whole milk

2 cups of espresso

Directions:

1. First, you brew espresso and add flavored sweetener of your choice (or omit) and coconut cream concentrate if you using it.

2. After which you pour into serving mugs.

3. Then you use espresso steamer, to steam milk and coconut oil to 140 degrees.

4. Finally, add to espresso and serve.

Coconut Peanut Butter Banana Protein Shake

Ingredients:

2 frozen bananas

2/3 cup of coconut milk

Dash guar gum (it is optional)

2-4 tablespoons of melted coconut oil (suitable for pre-workout)

2 serving vanilla protein powder

1 ¼ cups of water

2-4 tablespoons of Coconut Peanut Butter

Dash xanthan gum (it is optional)

Ice to taste (it is optional)

Directions:

1. First, you place the entire ingredients except coconut oil (if using) in blender and blend while you pouring coconut oil in a steady stream.

2. Then you blend until smooth and then serve.

Coconut Pumpkin Pie Smoothie

Ingredients:

2 bananas (fresh or frozen)

2 dashes of cinnamon

2 tablespoons of coconut oil (melted)

½ cup of pumpkin puree

1 cup of coconut milk

2 teaspoons of honey

Directions:

1. First, you combine pumpkin puree, banana, coconut milk, cinnamon, and honey in a blender.

2. After which you blend on high until well mixed and smooth.

3. Then while the blender is still running, you slowly pour in the coconut oil.

4. Finally, you pour in a glass and garnish with a sprinkle of cinnamon.

5. Enjoy!

Coconut Smoothie

Ingredients:

2 cups of water

2 tablespoons of Virgin coconut oil

6-8 tablespoons of coconut flour (feel free to put more if you want it thicker)

20-24 ice cubes

2-4 tablespoons of protein powder (preferably from goat's milk)

2 teaspoons of pure vanilla extract

2 tablespoons of flax seeds ground

Directions:

1. First, you place the entire ingredients in a blender and process at high speed until well combined.

You may require more or less of ice, depending on how you could want your smoothie to be.

Coconut Tropical Bliss Smoothie

Tips:

When you want to serve, you may sprinkle with dried coconut or even add a slice of pineapple to the glass.

Ingredients:

Almond Milk:

3 cups of distilled water

1 cup of raw almonds

Mix INS:

Fresh pineapple

2 tablespoons of coconut oil

Frozen bananas

Coconut cream (concentrate to taste)

Directions:

1. First, you blend nut milk in a high-speed blender.

2. After which you add remaining ingredients and blend until thoroughly mixed.

3. Then you adjust ingredients to your desired taste and thickness.

Coco nutty Green Smoothie

Ingredients:

4 HUGE handfuls of spinach

½ teaspoon of cinnamon

2 tablespoons of coconut oil

4 bananas (frozen)

2 cups of milk (raw is best)

2 teaspoons of vanilla

Directions:

1. First, you add the entire ingredients into a blender.

2. After which you blend until mixed.

3. Then you serve in a tall glass.

Creamy Coconut Cinnamon Smoothie

Tips:

1. I suggest you use coconut milk or fresh raw milk for this recipe.

2. Feel free to add natural sweetener as well, such as banana or a fresh pineapple, which gives it a nice tropical twist!

Ingredients:

2 medium frozen banana

1 teaspoon of vanilla extract

2 teaspoons of virgin coconut oil

3 cups of milk

2 heaping teaspoons of coconut cream concentrate

Dashes of cinnamon

Directions:

1. First, you place milk, banana, coconut cream concentrate, vanilla and cinnamon in blender.

2. After which you blend on high for about 30 seconds or until ingredients are well combined.

3. Then you slowly drizzle the virgin coconut oil into the mixture.

Dark Chocolate Raspberry Custard Smoothie

Ingredients:

4 tablespoons of organic cocoa powder (or preferably more to taste)

4-8 soy-free pastured egg yolks

1 teaspoon of organic vanilla extract

2 frozen bananas, for additional creaminess (it is optional)

3 cups of raw milk, plain kefir (preferably homemade, or coconut milk)

4 tablespoons of virgin coconut oil, melted (or preferably more to taste)

2 tablespoons of raw honey

Dashes of real sea salt

3 cups of organic frozen raspberries

Directions:

1. First, you blend all but the frozen ingredients until smooth.

2. After which you add fruit and blend to desired consistency.

3. Then you adjust all ingredients to taste and enjoy!

CONCLUSION

After spending a season drinking the nourishing smoothie found in this Thyroid healing smoothie recipe book, you will find yourself recovering faster and it will help you Maintain optimal performance and adjustment.

Take advantage of these healthy and delicious smoothie provided for you in this book.

I suggest you give it a trial.

www.ingramcontent.com/pod-product-compliance
Lightning Source LLC
Chambersburg PA
CBHW081729100526
44591CB00016B/2551